Into the Next Millennium

Medicine

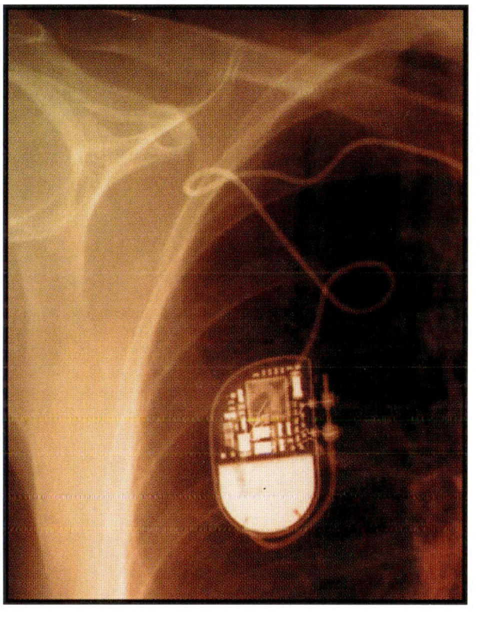

Deborah Cannarella

Jane Fournier

The Rourke Press
Vero Beach, Florida

Photo credits

Photographs © copyright: Agence France Presse/Corbis-Bettmann, p. 22–23 and 31 bottom; AP/Wide World Newsfeatures, p. 19 bottom, 21 bottom (John Chadwick), 26 bottom (Wilfredo Lee); Archive Photos, p. 19 top; Baxter Laboratories, p. 26 top; Bayer Co., p. 13 bottom; Corbis, pp. 8 bottom (David Lees), 17 bottom (Owen Franken); Corbis-Bettman, p. 6 bottom (Trong Jim Tchou), 9 top, 10 bottom, 11 top, 12 top; Criscola Design, p. 29 (Michelle Hurteau); Francis A. Countway Library of Medicine, p. 17 top (Rare Books and Special Collections); GE Medical Systems, p. 20 top; Hewlett Packard Co., p. 25 left; Hulton-Deutsch Collections/Corbis, pp. 15 bottom, 16 top, 18 bottom; Intuitive Surgical, pp. 23 bottom and 27 both (1998); NASA, p. 30–31; North Wind Picture Archive, pp. 4 top and 11 bottom, 4 middle and 10 top right, 6 top, 7 top, 10 top left, 12 middle (Edelfelt); Novartis Pharmaceuticals Corp., p. 24 top; PhotoDisc, pp. 2 and 18 top right, 23 top, 28 top left, 30; PhotoEdit, p. 28 bottom (David Young-Wolff); Photo Researchers, Inc., p. 16 middle (A. Barrington Brown/Science Source); Rainbow, pp. 16 bottom (R. Feldmann/D. McCoy), 20 bottom (Hank Morgan); Robert Lisak, p. 25 right; Siemens, p. 14 top; St. Jude Medical, Cardiac Rhythm Management Division, p. 18 top left; Stock Montage, Inc., pp. 4 bottom (Charles Walker Collection), 4–5 and 7 bottom (Mundinus), 8 top, 9 bottom, 13 middle, 15 top; U.S. National Library of Medicine, pp. 12 bottom, 24 bottom; Underwood & Underwood/Corbis-Bettman, p. 14 bottom; Yale Medicine publications, p. 13 top, 21 top (Robert Lisak), 23 middle (Robert Lisak). All cover and introduction page images PhotoDisc.

Printed in the United States of America

An Editorial Directions Book
Book design and production by Criscola Design

Library of Congress Cataloging-in-Publication Data

Cannarella, Deborah.
Medicine / Deborah Cannarella. Jane Fournier.
p. cm. — (Into the next millennium)
Summary : Surveys the history of medicine from ancient times through the present day and speculates about future medical discoveries and innovative treatments.
ISBN 1-57103-274-6
1. Medicine—History Juvenile Literature. [1. Medicine—History.] I. Fournier, Jane, 1955– . II. Title. III. Series.
R133.5.C26 1999
610'.9—dc21 99-25472
CIP

Introduction

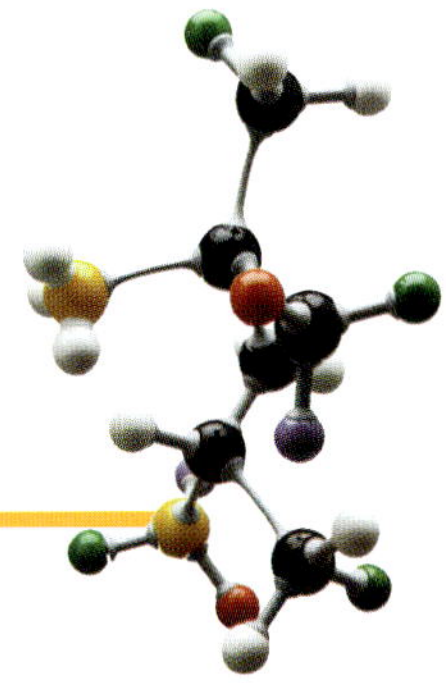

The history of the human race is a story of great discoveries and amazing achievements. Since ancient times, people have found creative solutions to problems, met impossible challenges, and turned visions into reality. Each of these remarkable people—and each of their contributions—changed the world they lived in forever. Together, they created the world we know and live in today.

The six books in this series—*Medicine, Transportation, Communication, Exploration, Engineering,* and *Sports*—present a timeline of the great discoveries and inventions that have shaped our world. As you travel from ancient to modern times, you will discover the many ways in which people have worked to heal sickness, shape materials, share information, explore strange places, and achieve new goals. Although they worked with many different tools, their goal was always the same: to improve our quality of life.

As we enter the twenty-first century, we will continue to build on what each generation of people before us has created and discovered. With the knowledge they have given us, we will discover new ways to build, heal, communicate, discover, and achieve. We will continue to change the world in ways we can only begin to imagine.

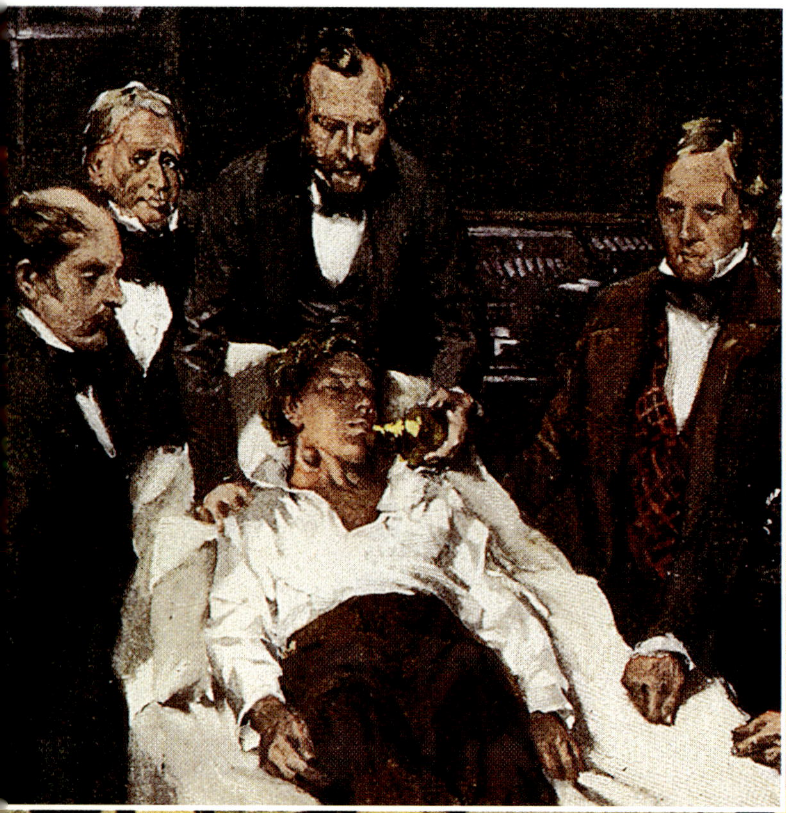

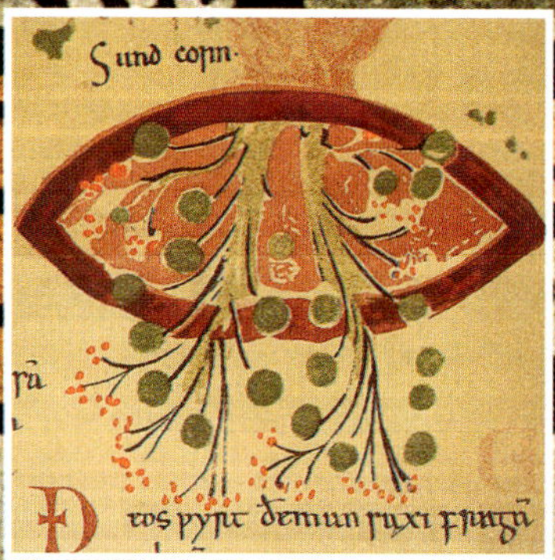

*From the **Past**...*

2700 B.C.

In prehistoric and native cultures throughout the world, **herbs and other plant materials** were applied to the body of a person with an illness or given to a patient internally to relieve colds, fevers, wounds, and stomachaches. Plant drugs were first written about in China in 2700 B.C.

The bark of the willow tree contains salicin, a chemical related to the pain-killing substance found in today's aspirin.

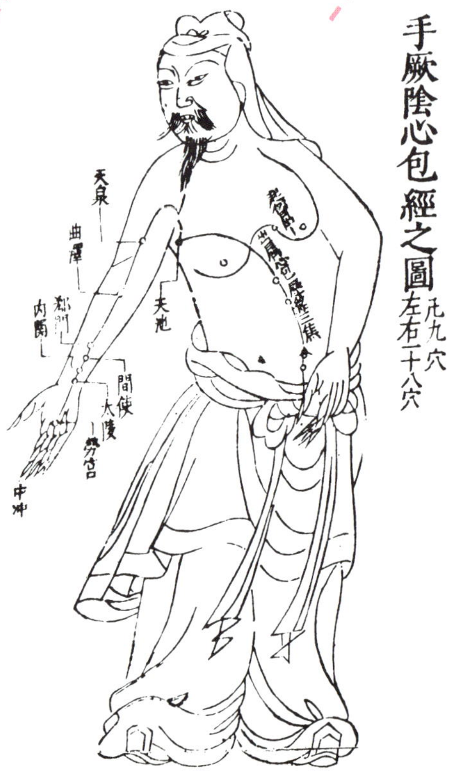

2500 B.C.

For more than 2,000 years, the Chinese have practiced **acupuncture**. Small needles are inserted into areas of the body to relieve pain, cure disease, and improve health. Today in China, acupuncture is used to numb a patient's pain during surgery.

Many prehistoric people believed disease was caused by evil spirits trapped inside the sick person's head. To cure the patient, they cut a hole in the person's skull to let the evil spirits escape. This practice is called **trepanning**, or trephining.

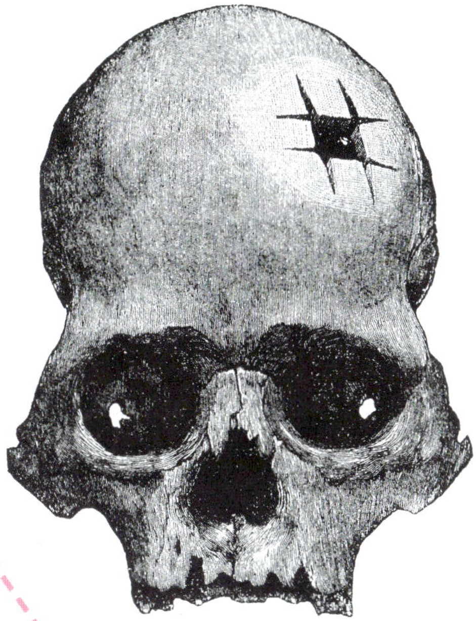

During the Middle Ages (fifth through fifteenth centuries), people believed that blood-sucking worms called leeches would cure illness. In a practice known as bloodletting, or bleeding, doctors attached leeches to a patient's body to draw out diseases in the blood.

1543

In 1543, Andreas Vesalius wrote and illustrated the first textbook of **anatomy**—based on what he learned from the dissection (cutting and examining) of human corpses. The ancient Greek writings about the human body had been based on the dissections of animals.

1575

French physician Ambroise Paré made drawings of **artificial hands, arms, and legs**. Paré, who was the first to use stitches during amputations—the removal of limbs—is known as the Father of Modern Surgery. He also invented artificial teeth and artificial eyes made of gold and silver.

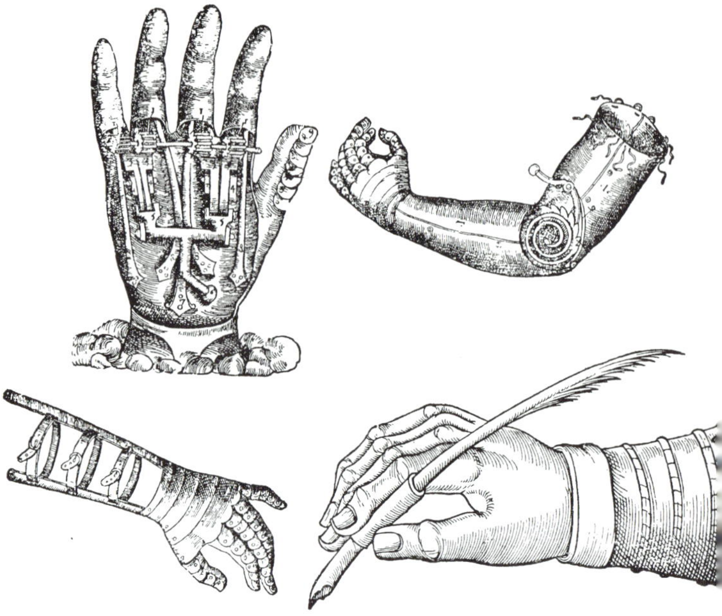

In 1714, German physicist Daniel Gabriel Fahrenheit made the first mercury thermometer. Today's digital mercury thermometers register the temperature with liquid crystal displays (LCDs).

1590

Galileo Galilei invented the **thermometer** in 1590. In 1612, his friend Sanctorius redesigned the instrument to measure human body temperature. The open end of a tube containing water was held in the patient's mouth for about 20 minutes. Sanctorius counted the bubbles in the warming water. The higher the patient's fever, the more bubbles—and the higher in the tube the cooled water would rise.

The Harrington "Erado" clockwork dental drill was made in about 1864. When the drill was fully wound, the dentist could drill for up to two minutes.

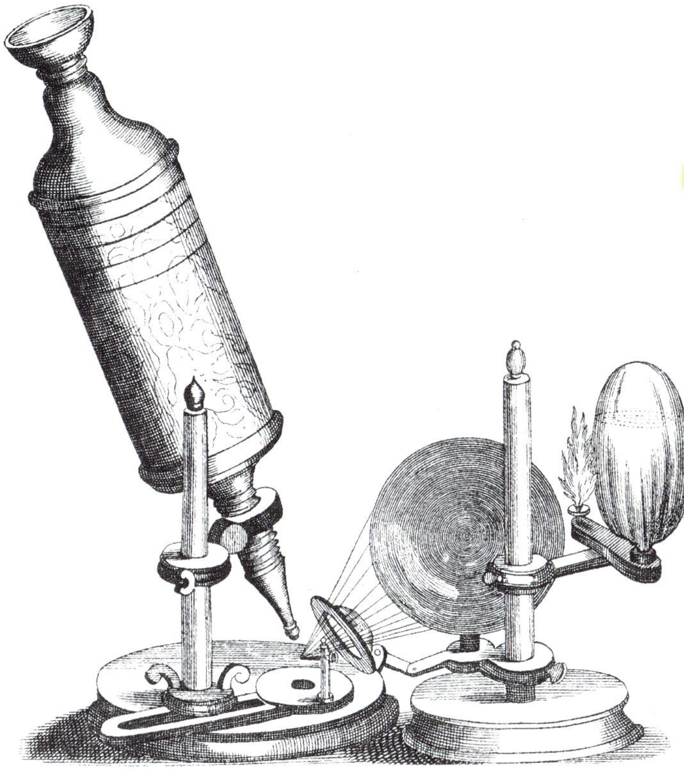

1660

A Dutchman named Antonie van Leeuwenhoek ground his own lenses and built fine, single-lens **microscopes**. He examined pond water, cloth, bees, flies, and blood. He became famous for his discoveries and his detailed descriptions of bacteria and one-celled animals.

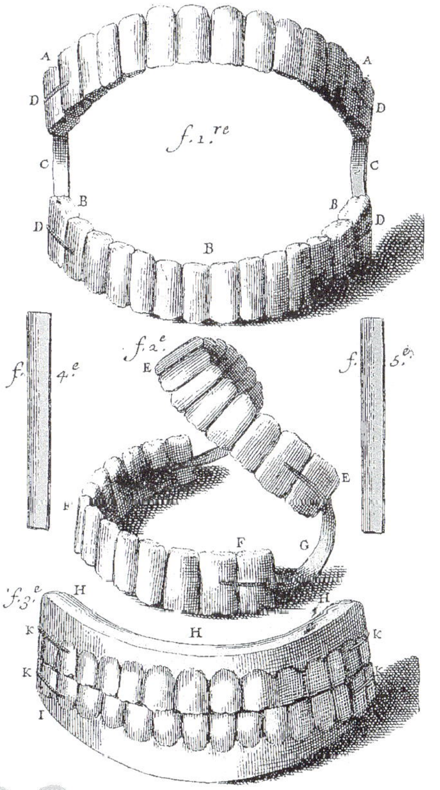

1780

The first **false teeth**—used in Italy about 2,500 years ago—were made of ivory, bone, gold, or human teeth. In the late 1700s, dentists started making dentures from porcelain (above). The first full set of false teeth similar to those used today was made in France in the 1780s.

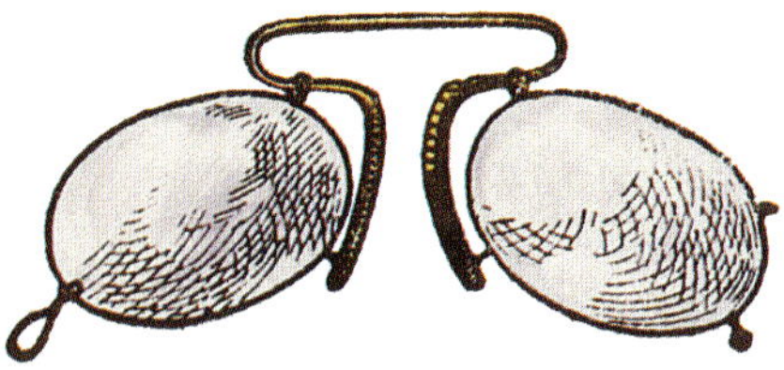

1784

Early **eyeglasses** helped only farsighted people, who could not see objects close to their eyes. Eyeglasses for near-sighted people were invented in about 1500. In 1784, Benjamin Franklin combined the two kinds of lenses to make the first bifocals (above).

1796

Doctor Edward Jenner of England, cured eight-year-old James Phipps of the serious disease known as smallpox. Jenner scraped the pus from the hand of a woman infected with cowpox into scratches on the boy's arm. The doctor believed that exposure to a similar disease would help the body resist infection. By 1800, about 100,000 people had received Jenner's **smallpox vaccine**.

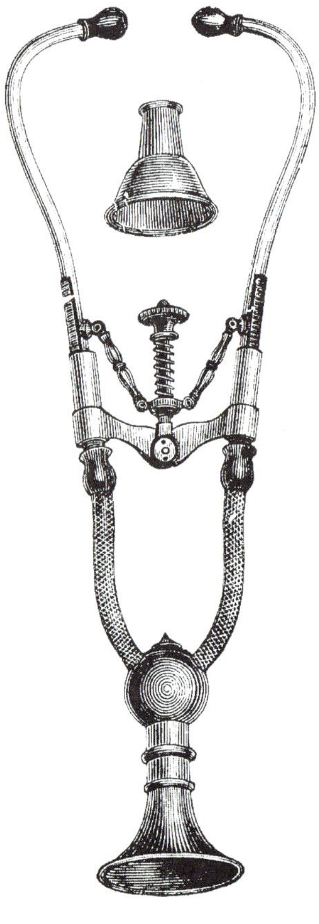

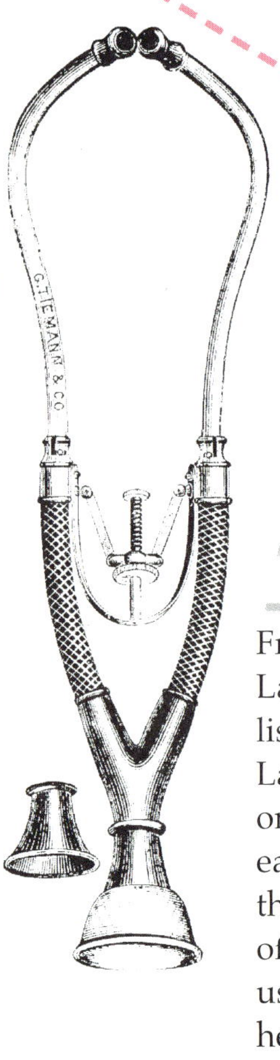

1819

French physician René-Théophile-Hyacinthe Laënnec was watching children tap on a board and listen to the sound that traveled through the wood. Laënnec rolled a piece of paper into a tube. He held one end against a patient's chest and the other to his ear. He discovered that he could hear every beat of the patient's heart! Laënnec made wooden models of the invention he called a **stethoscope**. Doctors use stethoscopes to listen to the sounds made by the hearts, lungs, blood vessels—and even the heartbeat of a baby in its mother's womb.

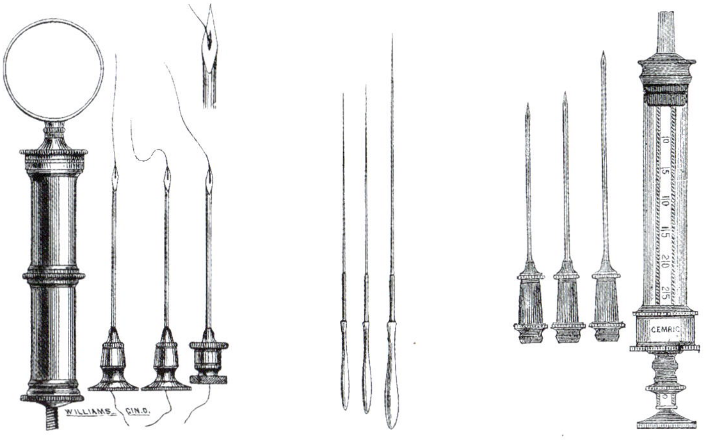

1850

Syringes were first used in ancient India, China, and North Africa. In about 1850, French surgeon Charles Gabriel Pravaz first used a syringe fitted with a sharp, hollow needle to inject drugs. Today's syringes consist of a hollow glass or plastic barrel and a plunger.

In 1796, the German doctor Samuel Hahnemann introduced the principles of homeopathy. This system is based on the idea that a substance that causes an illness can be used to cure that illness. Homeopathy—practiced in India since 1810—is considered an alternative type of medicine in the United States.

1842

In 1842, Doctor Crawford W. Long first used the gas ether as an **anesthesia** to dull the pain of his patient during an operation. In 1844, dentist Horace Wells began using nitrous oxide (also called laughing gas) in his practice. Patients inhaled the gases through a face mask. The Letheon ether inhaler of 1847 was a glass jar filled with ether-soaked sponges, through which air was drawn as the patient inhaled.

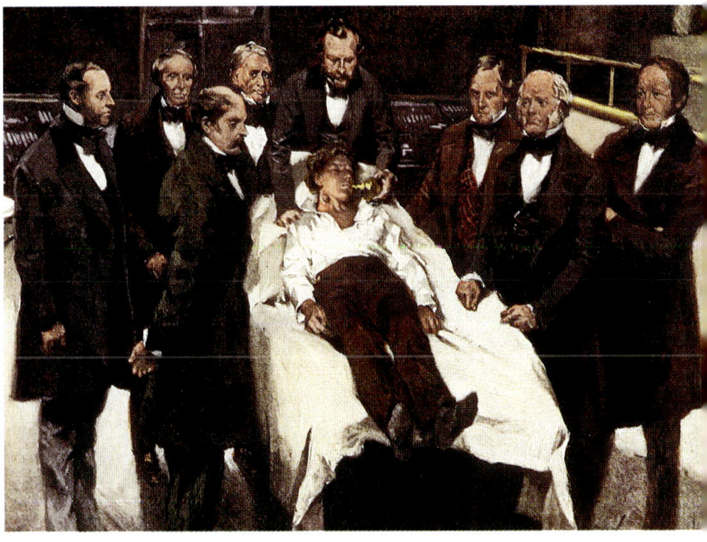

The word *hypnosis* is from the Greek word *hypnos*, which means "sleep." Before gas anesthesia was available, Scottish physician James Esdaille used hypnosis—a method of creating a sleeplike state—to rid his patients of pain.

1865

Scottish surgeon Joseph Lister wanted to keep his patients from becoming infected by germs during operations. In 1865, he used a steam spray of carbolic acid, a substance used for cleaning sewers, to protect and clean surgical openings. The number of deaths during surgery decreased greatly. Lister had discovered the first **antiseptic**.

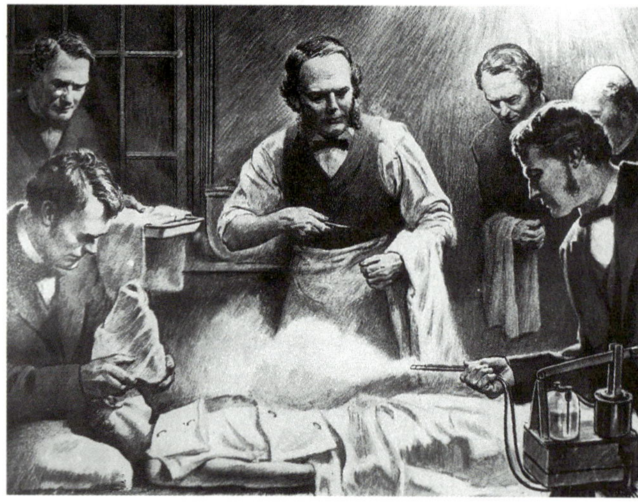

In 1952, Jonas E. Salk developed a vaccine against polio, a disease that crippled and killed children and adults. Salk later worked to develop a vaccine for HIV, the virus that causes AIDS.

1884

In 1884, Louis Pasteur developed the **vaccine against rabies**—a deadly virus transmitted through animal bites. Pasteur dried the spinal cords of infected animals to make a liquid. Although Pasteur had never tested his vaccine on humans, a mother who was afraid that her infected son would die asked for his help. After treatment, the boy was cured.

1891

Blood pressure is measured by slowly applying force to the patient's skin until the flow of blood is stopped and the pulse disappears—and then releasing the force. The instrument that applies the force and measures the blood flow and pulse is called a **sphygmomanometer.** It was invented by Samuel von Basch.

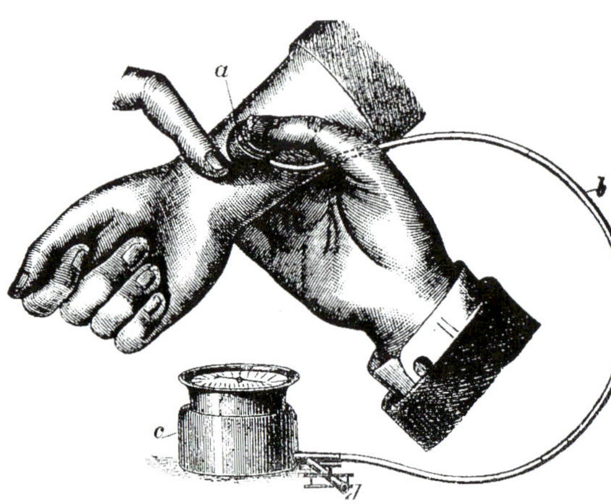

1895

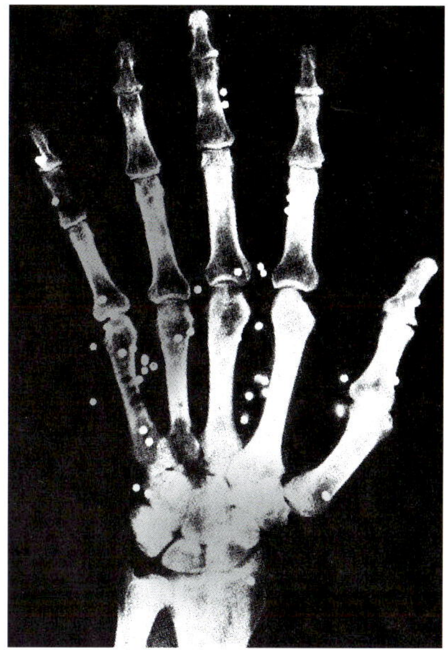

While researching electricity, Sir William Crookes created a vacuum tube in which invisible rays created a glow. In 1895, Sir Wilhelm Conrad Roentgen discovered that even when the tube was covered with black cloth, the invisible rays passed through. When he put his hand in front of the rays, he could see the outline of his bones! Roentgen called the rays **X rays** because he didn't know what they were. Before the X ray was invented, there was no way to see inside the human body without surgery.

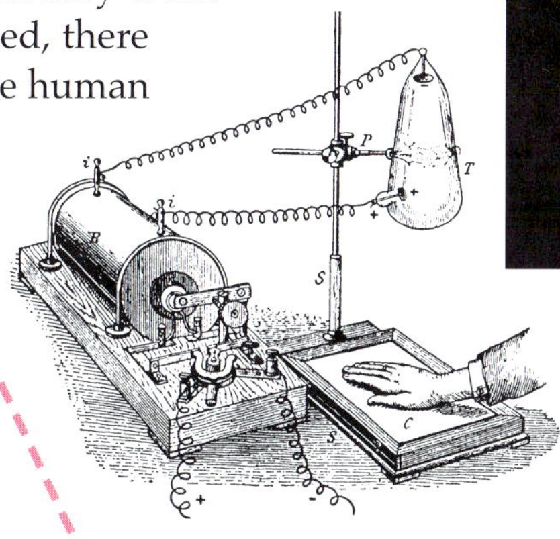

X rays are used to destroy cancerous tissue, to discover broken bones or tumors, and to reveal problems such as blockages and ulcers.

1899

More than 2,000 years ago, physicians in ancient Greece and Rome made a tea of the bark and leaves of willow trees to relieve pain and fever. French scientist Henry Leroux identified salicin as the pain-relieving substance in willow. German chemist Felix Hofmann gave his father a compound of salicin to relieve his father's arthritis. Hofman's employer, Friedrich Bayer and Company, first marketed the substance—which it named **aspirin**—in 1899. Today, aspirin is one of the world's most widely used medicines.

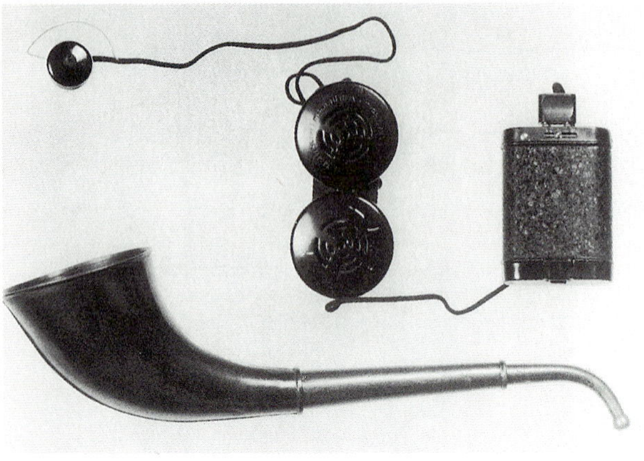

1902

The ear trumpet (bottom), the earliest **hearing aid,** was a tapered tube with a large opening at one end to collect sound and a small opening at the other to insert into the ear. The first battery-powered hearing aid was developed in about 1902. Large batteries were carried in boxes or strapped to the legs of the wearers. When transistors and magnetic microphones were first available in the 1950s, hearing aids became smaller and more powerful (top). They could be carried in a pocket or disguised as jewelry.

In 1985, hearing aids were made with microchips. Modern models, worn behind the earlobe, can barely be seen.

1903

Doctor Willem Einthoven built a string galvanometer—a horseshoe-shaped magnet with a wire—to measure the electricity in the human body. He later invented the machine called an **electrocardiograph,** or EKG. Doctors use the EKG to see if the heart is working properly. Today's machine is similar to Einthoven's original design, but is much smaller and improved.

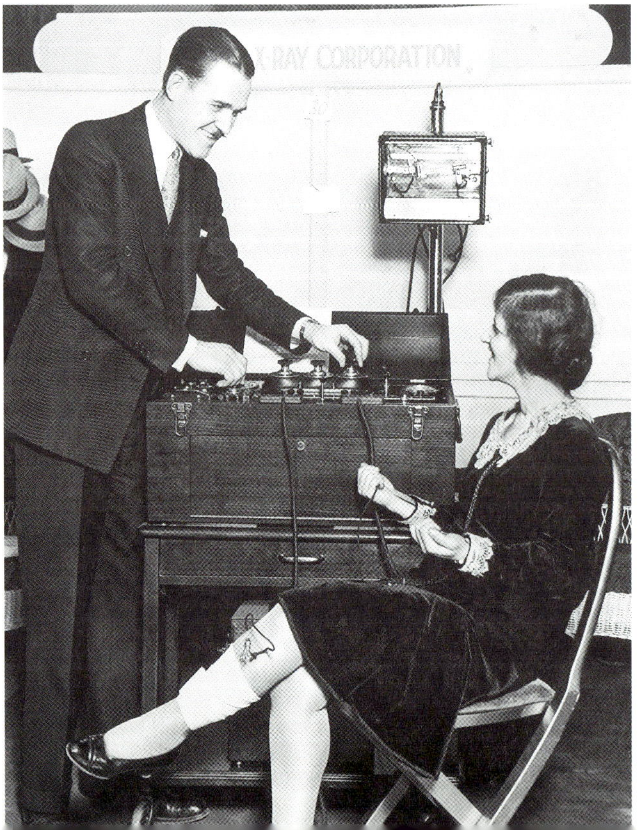

The first EKG weighed 800 pounds (360 kg) and could not be moved to the hospital to be used—so the hospital ran wire to Einthoven's lab instead!

In 1920, Earle Dickson invented the first Band-Aid. He placed squares of cotton gauze along the sticky side of a roll of adhesive tape. Every time he wanted a bandage, he simply cut one from the roll. Dickson's employer, Johnson & Johnson, soon began producing the now world-famous Band-Aids.

1928

While doing research, Scottish scientist Sir Alexander Fleming was growing staph germs (a type of bacteria) in a petri dish. One day, he noticed a strange mold in the dish. He also noticed that the germs around the mold were dead. He realized that a substance in the mold was destroying the bacteria. He called this substance **penicillin.** In 1944, it began to be manufactured to fight diseases.

The type of mold in which penicillin was found is commonly found on old bread. Ancient Egyptians used the mold from bread to treat wounds.

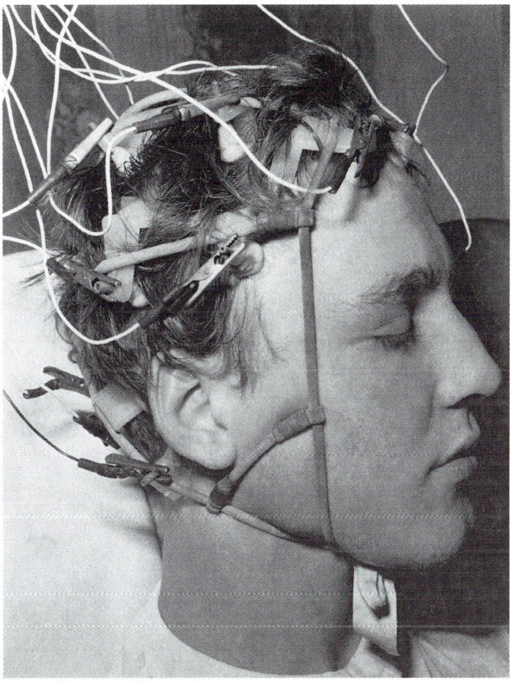

1929

The **electroencephalograph,** or EEG, was invented by German scientist Hans Berger. This device measures and records the electrical activity in the brain. Doctors place sets of electrodes on a patient's scalp. Each set sends a signal to the EEG. The signals appear as a wave pattern on a printout. The EEG helps doctors find tumors and study head injuries and diseases of the nervous system.

1933

An electron is one of the particles in an atom. Cathode rays are streams of high-speed electrons. In 1924, French scientist Louis de Broglie discovered how to use cathode rays to increase the power of a microscope. In 1933, German engineer Ernst Ruska built the first **electron microscope.** This powerful device could magnify objects more than 100,000 times, allowing doctors to identify bacteria that cause disease. With today's electron microscopes, scientists view molecules and some atoms.

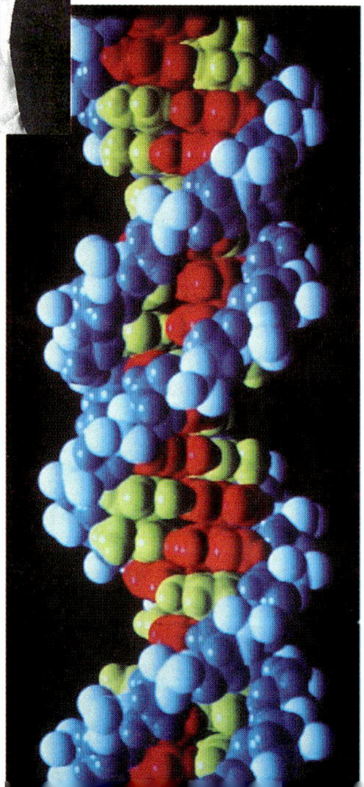

1953

Every plant and animal on earth is composed of cells. Each cell contains genes, which carry the codes for specific traits, such as eye color and height. Genes are made of **deoxyribonucleic acid** (DNA).

In 1953, Francis Crick and James Watson discovered the DNA molecule. They described it as a double helix—a spiral ladder made up of two intertwined chains. Their discovery has helped scientists to treat many diseases, such as diabetes and cancer. DNA evidence also helps police identify criminals.

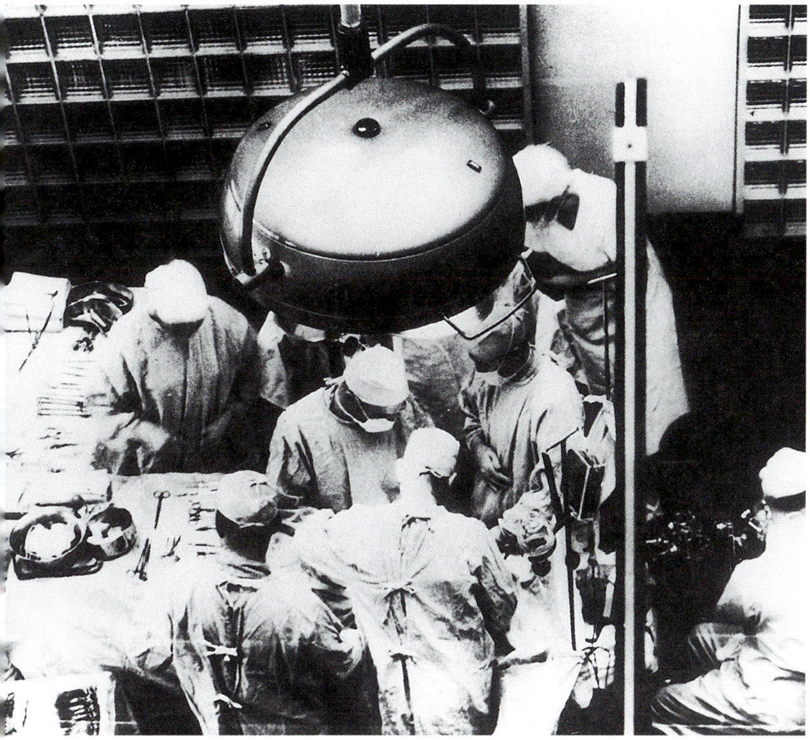

1954

The first successful **organ transplant** was performed by American surgeon Joseph Murray. He transplanted a kidney from the body of a boy to the body of the boy's twin brother. Today, thousands of kidneys are transplanted each year. Eye tissue, bone marrow, and at least twenty other types of organs—including hearts and livers—can now be successfully transplanted to help or cure patients.

1957

Ultrasound scanners are tools for exploring the human body with sound waves. The sound waves strike the organs in the body and produce echoes. The echoes display a picture on a screen. Doctors use ultrasound scanners to locate tumors and blockages and also to examine babies inside the mothers' wombs. In 1957, scientist Ian Donald and engineer Tom Brown constructed the first scanner. Today's ultrasound scanners produce very clear, high-resolution images.

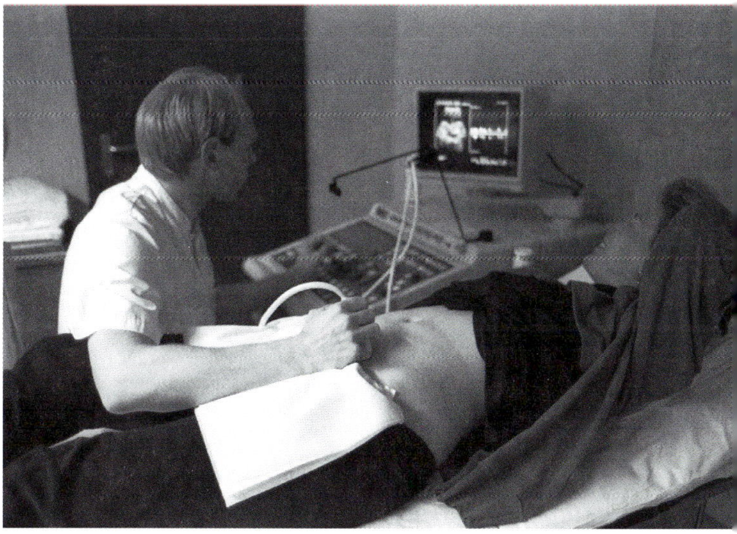

1958

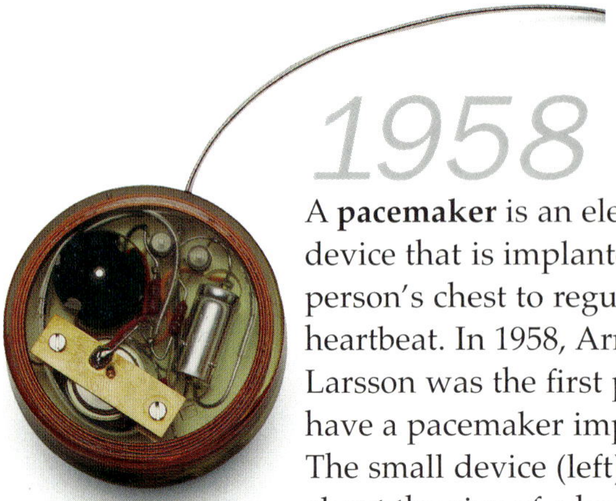

A **pacemaker** is an electronic device that is implanted in a person's chest to regulate the heartbeat. In 1958, Arne Larsson was the first person to have a pacemaker implanted. The small device (left) was about the size of a hockey puck, weighed almost 3 ounces (93 g), and was powered by a battery with a one-year life span. Today's pacemakers (right) are microcomputers that weigh as little as 0.5 ounce (16 g) and last up to 20 years. More than 2 million people use pacemakers today.

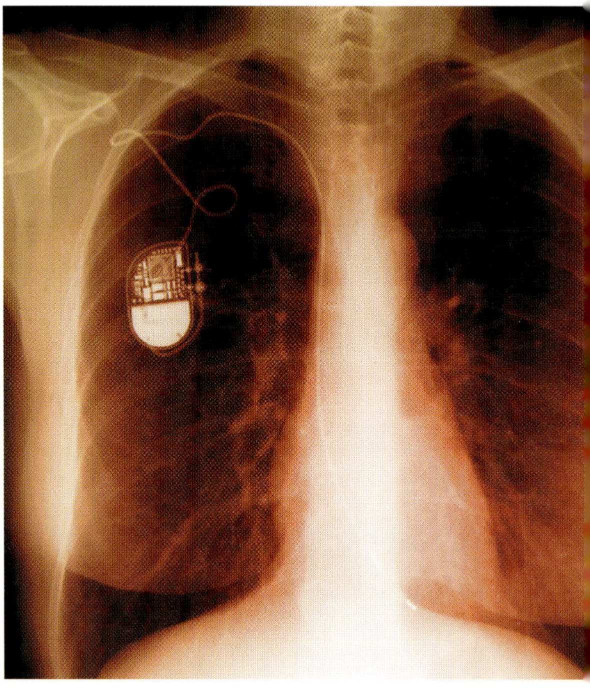

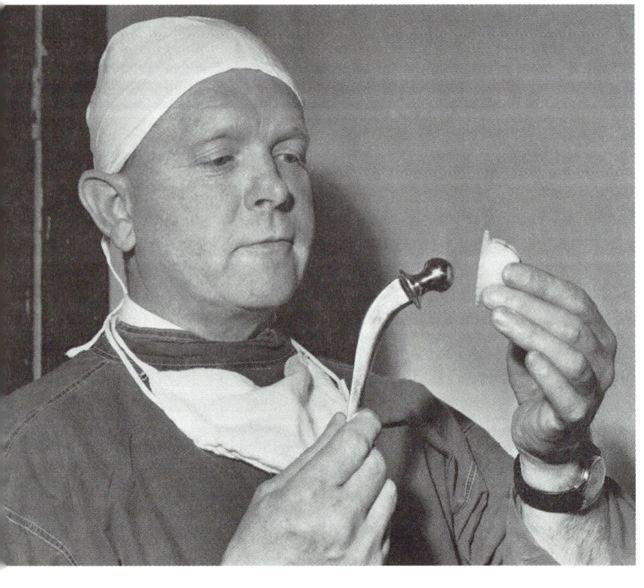

1960

In 1960, Sir John Charnley of England made the first successful joint replacement. He created an **artificial hip** by gluing two pieces—one metal and one plastic—into a patient using bone cement. Today, more than 120,000 artificial hips and 240,000 artificial knees are placed in patients each year. The surgery is still based on Charnley's original idea. Instead of metal, the joints are now made of titanium alloys, which match human bone more closely. Feet, shoulders, elbows, and hands can also be replaced.

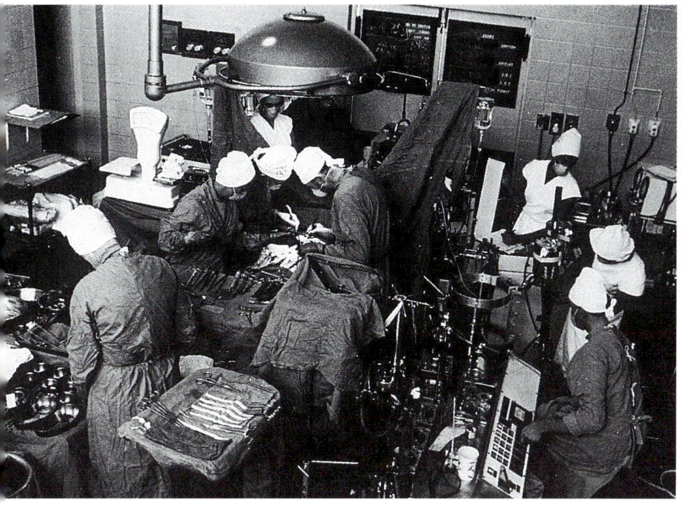

1967

The first successful human **heart transplant** was performed in 1967 by South African surgeon Christiaan Barnard. He transplanted the heart of a twenty-five-year-old woman who had died in a car accident into the body of a fifty-five-year-old man. Since then, thousands of heart transplants have been performed.

Many people give doctors permission to transplant their organs to other patients after they die. To meet the growing need for transplants, however, scientists are searching for ways to create artificial organs.

1968

The EEG, developed in 1929, measures the electrical activity of the brain using electrodes. The **magnetoencephalograph** (MEG) measures the magnetic and electrical activity of the brain using computer technology. The instrument, shown at right, takes pictures of the brain in action to locate the source of any problems. The MEG was first tested in 1968 by Dr. David Cohen.

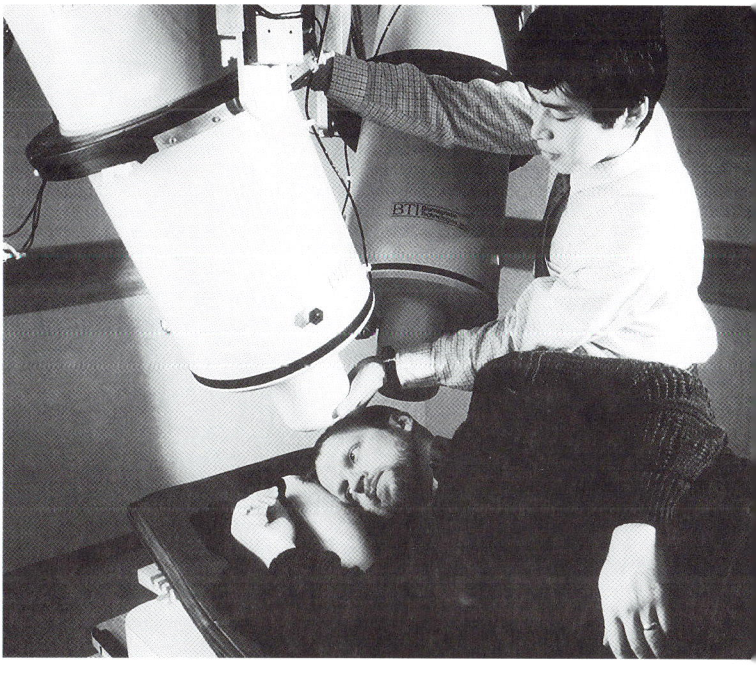

Computerized axial tomography (CAT) is a method of examining tumors with a tiny X-ray beam. The instrument was developed by Sir Godfrey Newbold Hounsfield, an electrical engineer, and was first tested in 1972. CAT scans are also known as CT scans.

1977

The **magnetic resonance imaging** (MRI) scanner uses radio signals to examine tissue in the body. These signals are then made into pictures. The pictures are much more detailed than pictures made with X-ray devices such as the CT scanner. Dr. Raymond Damadian tested his first scanner—the Indomitable—by producing the first image of a human chest in 1977. The Indomitable is now in the collection of the Smithsonian Institute in Washington, D.C.

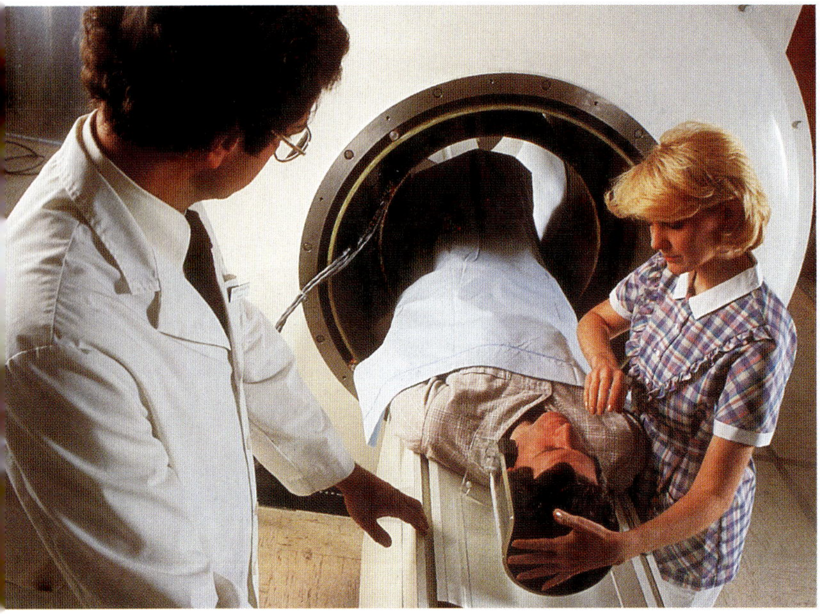

In 1977, researchers discovered the gene that makes **insulin,** an important human hormone. Scientists created an artificial form of the gene. They then used it to treat people with the disease diabetes. In the future, doctors hope to transplant healthy genes into people to replace the damaged genes that cause diseases.

In vitro fertilization (IVF) was developed to help women who were unable to become pregnant. The Latin words *in vitro* mean "in glass." Doctors remove an egg from a woman's ovary and fertilize the egg with a man's sperm in a petri dish in a laboratory. When the egg is fertilized, the doctors place the egg back in the woman's uterus, where it may grow into a baby. The first successful in vitro fertilization was performed in England in 1977. The baby's name was Louise Brown. Since then, thousands of babies have been born using the IVF method.

1995

In 1960, Theodore Maiman produced the first laser—a beam of red light so powerful that it could drill a hole through a diamond. Since 1995, doctors have been performing **laser eye surgery.** Scientists continue to work to develop laser techniques to help doctors perform many other types of delicate and complex operations.

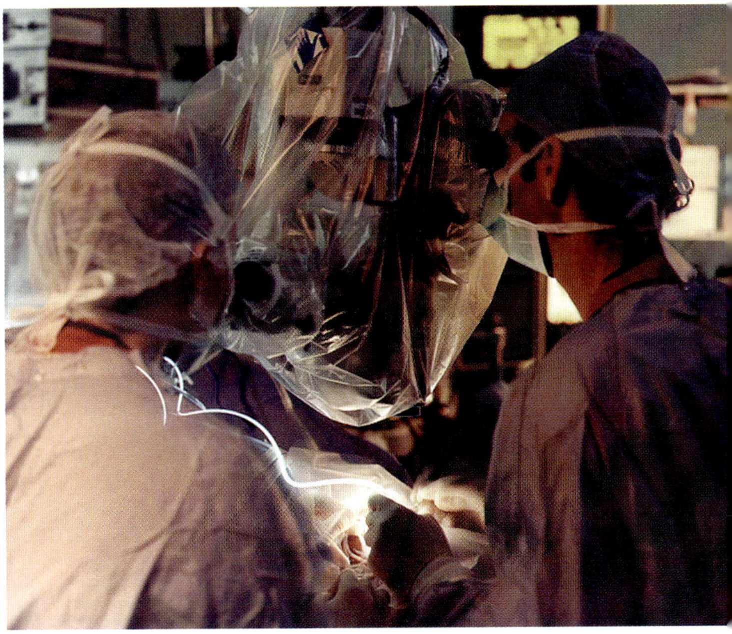

In China, some hospitals use laser light instead of acupuncture needles to treat patients. Low-powered laser beams are shot into the same points of the body where needles traditionally were inserted to treat disease.

1997

In 1997, a lamb named Dolly was the first mammal created in a laboratory through a method called **cloning.** Scientists transferred a sheep's cells into the unfertilized egg of another sheep. The egg was then placed in the uterus of a female sheep, which gave birth to the young lamb. Dolly is a clone—or exact copy—of the sheep that provided the cells. In 1998, scientists at the University of Hawaii cloned clones for the first time. They made more than 50 identical mice that are exact copies of their relatives.

Stitches are being replaced by fast-drying, nontoxic glues. One type is a painless, liquid bandage. The glue wears away as the skin heals. Another type of medical glue is for use during surgery—especially in places where stitches cannot now be used, such as the inner ear or blood-vessel walls.

...Into the **Future**

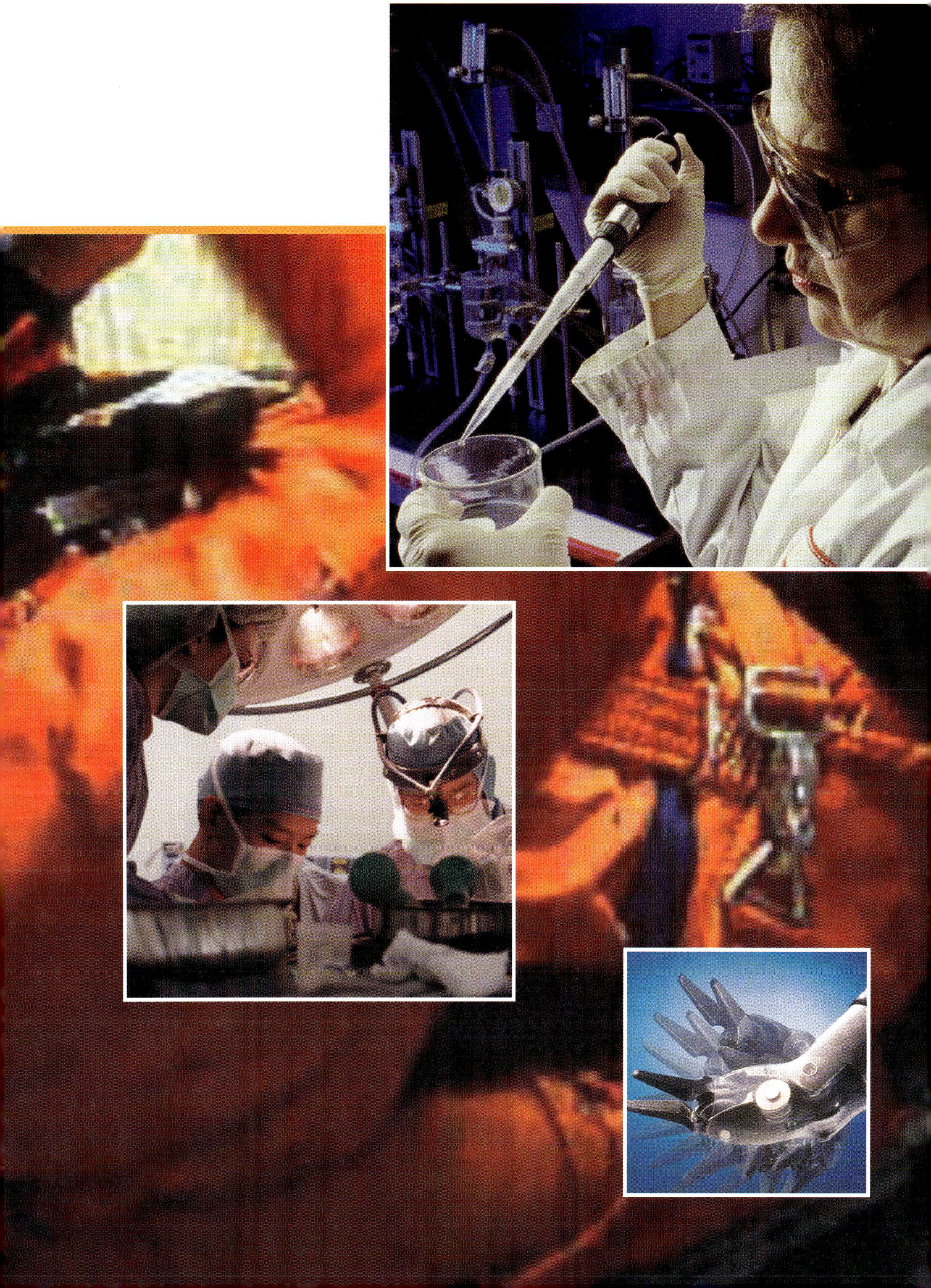

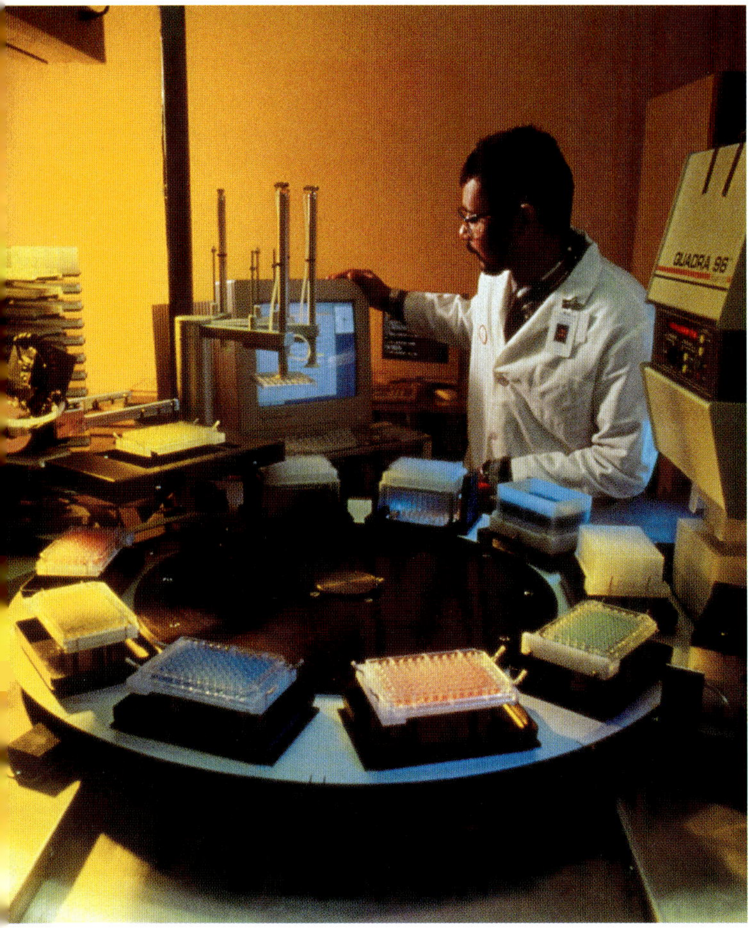

Genetic engineering. Genetic engineers insert new genes into plant and animal cells to make small, important changes in the way the organisms function. This technique may help scientists develop new medicines and find ways to repair or replace damaged genes that cause human disease.

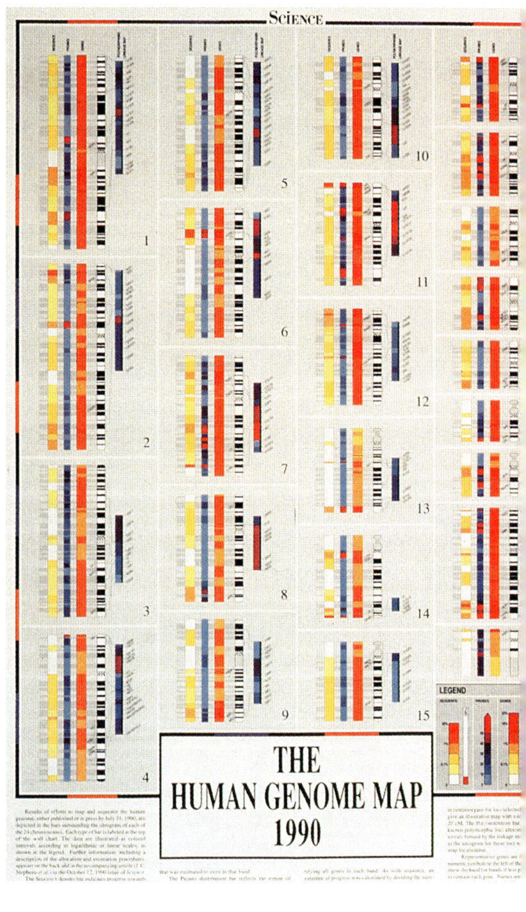

The Human Genome Project. By 2003, scientists expect to have a full, accurate map of the human chromosomes (the human genome). This map will show the locations and DNA patterns of the roughly 100,000 genes that determine a human's physical characteristics. With this information, genetic engineers hope to find new ways to treat serious diseases caused by damaged genes.

Computers in the operating room. Computers already deliver high-quality images of the patient to guide surgeons in the operating room. Eventually, computers may participate in the operations, too. Doctors are working with computer-guided magnets to make very small, precise incisions in sensitive organs, such as the brain. The magnets guide a small, flexible, metal-tipped probe along the path directed by the doctor.

High-resolution imagery. With the help of computers, medical instruments—such as the MRI and the ultrasound—can produce detailed, three-dimensional images of the body as it functions. Doctors hope that computers will soon help them take virtual-reality tours inside the body—to see the workings of major blood vessels, the brain, heart, and lungs. These advanced tools will help doctors locate tumors and diagnose disease without the need for surgery.

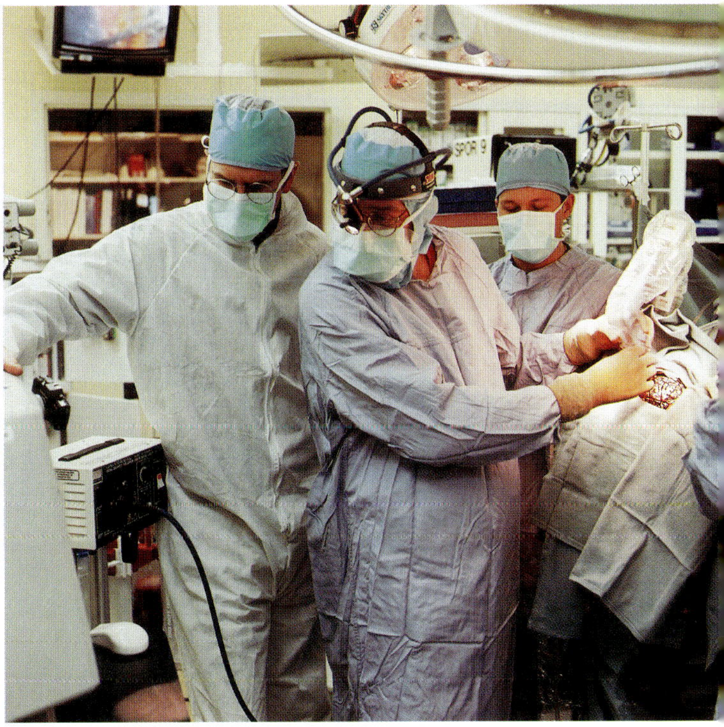

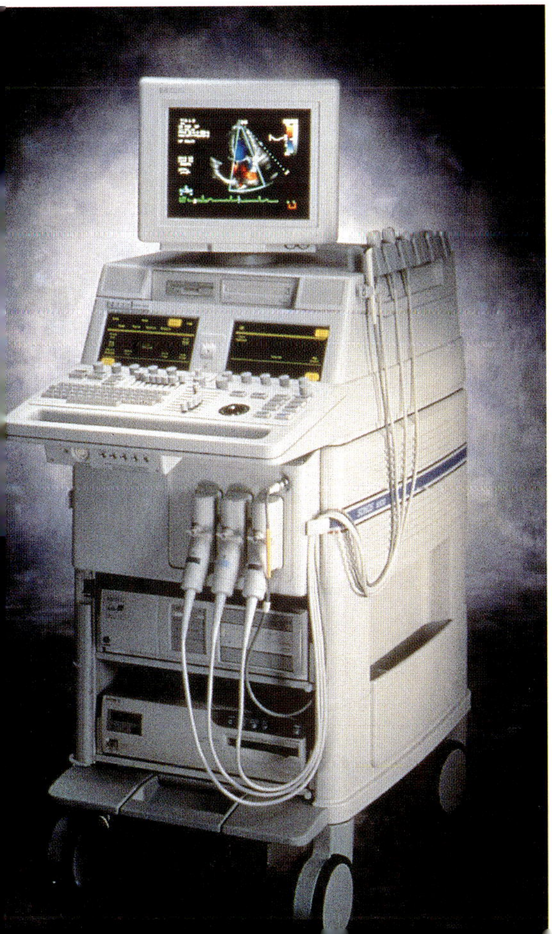

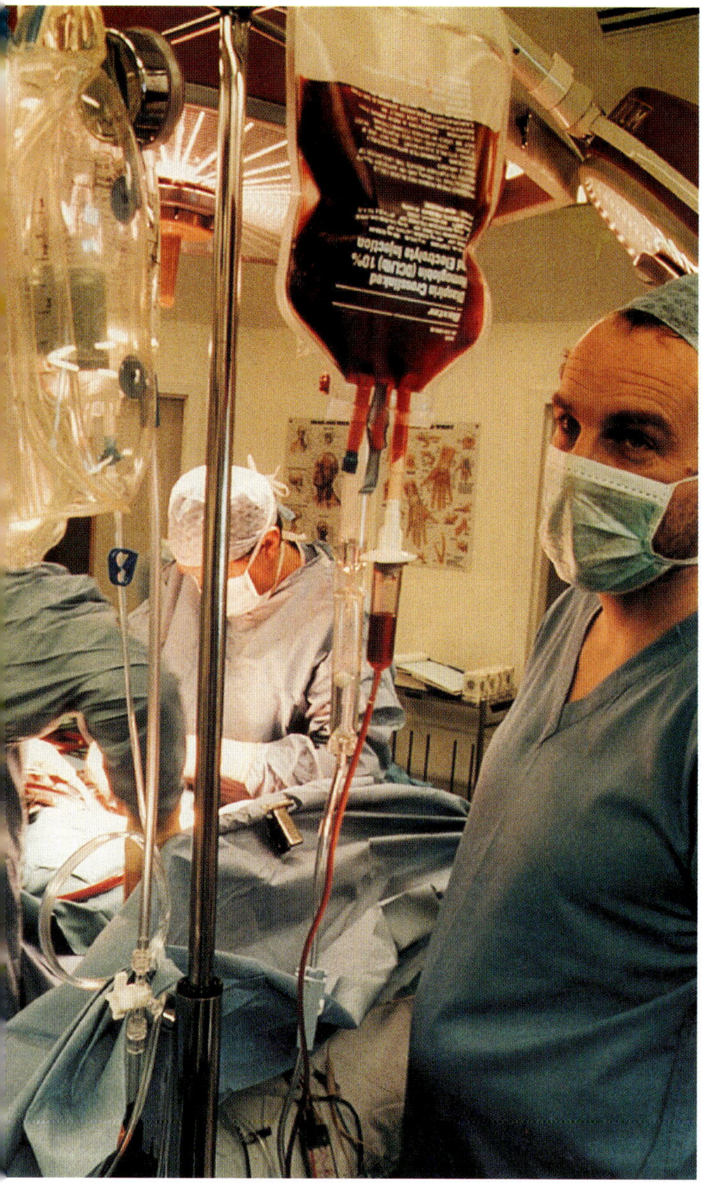

Artificial blood.
Artificial blood is being made from bioengineered (laboratory-constructed) animal products and from synthetic (artificial) compounds. Artificial blood may soon replace real blood in emergency cases and in surgery. It stays fresh longer than donated blood, matches any blood type, and does not carry disease-causing organisms, such as hepatitis and HIV.

Electrode implants.
People who are unable to use their limbs may soon use the electrical impulses created by their thoughts to control computers. Tiny electrodes implanted in their brains will help them communicate through e-mail, access the Internet, and perform various tasks—perhaps even move artificial limbs.

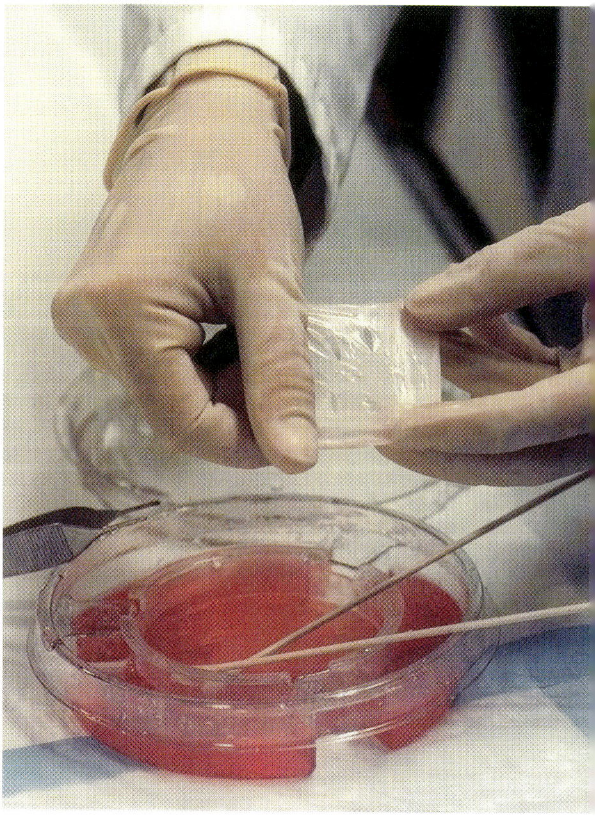

New artificial limbs with small, battery-powered, motorized joints can move as naturally as the limbs they replace. The joint motors are controlled by sensors that detect slight movements of the remaining muscles or tendons. By implanting tiny electrical sensors into nerves, scientists hope someday to create artificial limbs that will respond to nerve impulses.

Bioengineered skin. Skin is being made in the laboratory from human skin cells and animal collagen (protein tissue). Doctors hope to use this skin to heal wounds, burns, and areas affected by skin cancer. Because it is living tissue, bioengineered skin looks and behaves like real skin and blends with the patient's skin as it heals. It may also help patients with severe skin diseases to regrow healthy skin.

Remote-control surgery. Robots will soon assist doctors in surgery. In remote-surgery systems, a robot works at the operating table. The doctor directs the robot's movement from the other side of the room, watching the operation on a monitor. Motors in the robot's arms move sensitive instruments that enter the patient, making tiny cuts. With remote-control surgery, doctors will be able to operate, long distance, on patients in any part of the world.

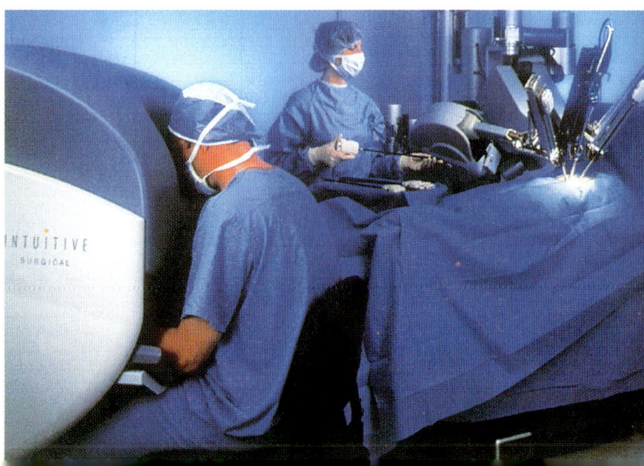

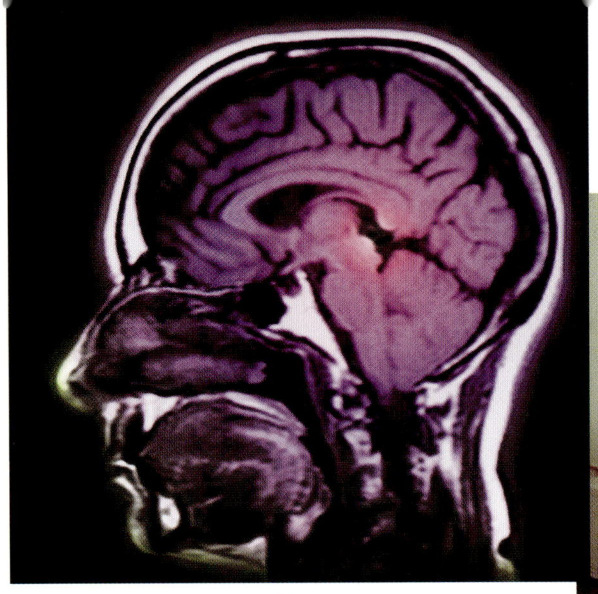

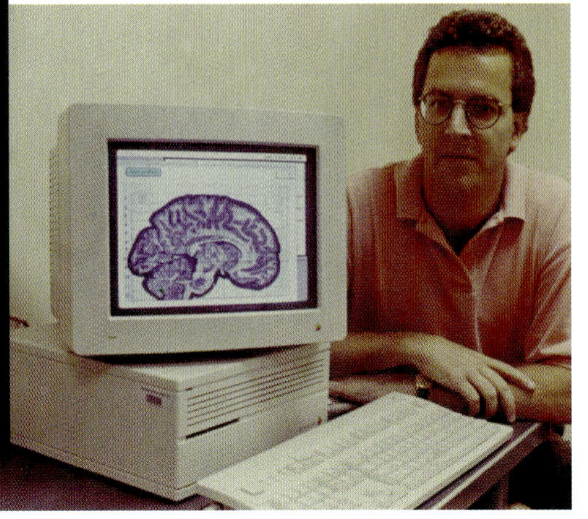

Computer access.
Medical information is being recorded, analyzed, and stored in electronic form. Through the Internet, doctors can access patient records, research materials, and medical images—and communicate with other scientists—anywhere in the world. Fast access to these resources will mean timely, accurate diagnoses and effective treatment plans.

Edible vaccines.
Genetic engineers have already grown potatoes that contain vaccines. They hope to produce other vegetables and fruits that will contain vaccines against childhood diseases. Edible vaccines would be easier to produce—and much easier to take. Scientists hope that edible vaccines will help reduce the numbers of infant deaths in many nations.

Artificial organ tissues.
One day, scientists hope to be able to grow heart, brain, liver, or other organ tissues from stem cells (cells in an early stage of development). Human stem cells can grow any type of cell in the human body—when given the correct chemical signals. Scientists are still working to understand these signals. They hope to be able to grow tissues to rebuild and perhaps replace organs damaged by injury or disease.

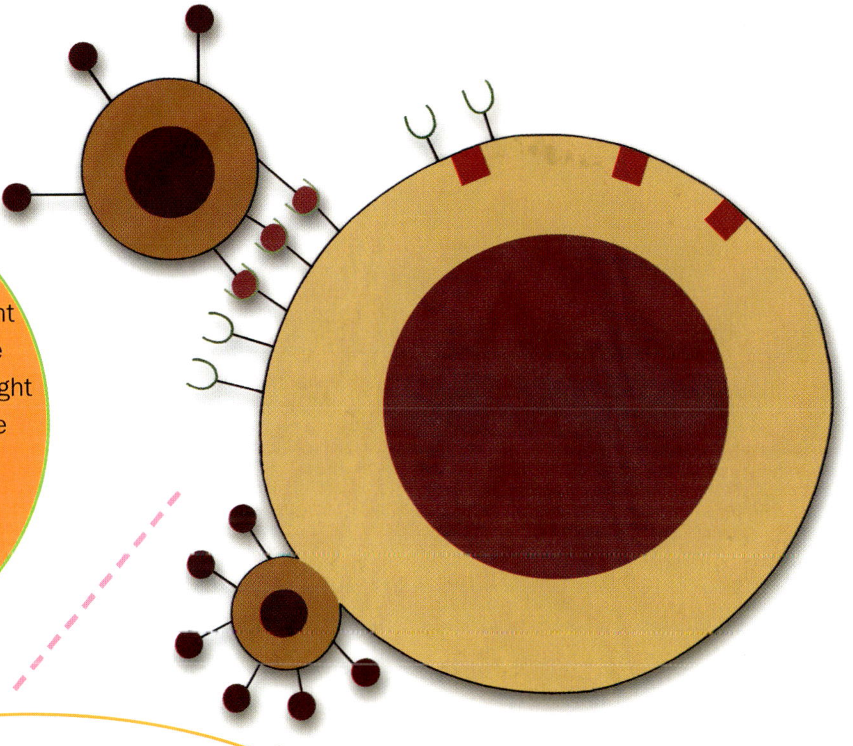

Many doctors believe that the human mind itself will play an important part in medical treatment. The mind's role in helping the body fight disease—the power of positive thinking—may be featured as a way to treat all types of illnesses and to improve overall health and well-being.

Smart drugs.
"Smart drugs" are viruses that are genetically engineered to recognize diseased cells within the body. They attack and kill only the diseased cells, leaving the healthy cells unharmed. Smart drugs have few known side effects. They are also able to reproduce, so they can be used as long-term therapy. Scientists hope that these drugs will provide better treatment for diseases such as HIV and cancer. In this drawing, a "smart" virus (top left) attacks a human cell (right) infected with HIV.

The rain forests.

With help from native healers, scientists are discovering new plant-based drugs in the South American rain forests. They expect to develop new medicines from the leaves, bark, sap, seeds, and wood of plants. As scientists learn more about diseases and as new diseases develop, the rain forests—and many of its nearly extinct species—will provide important information for cures.

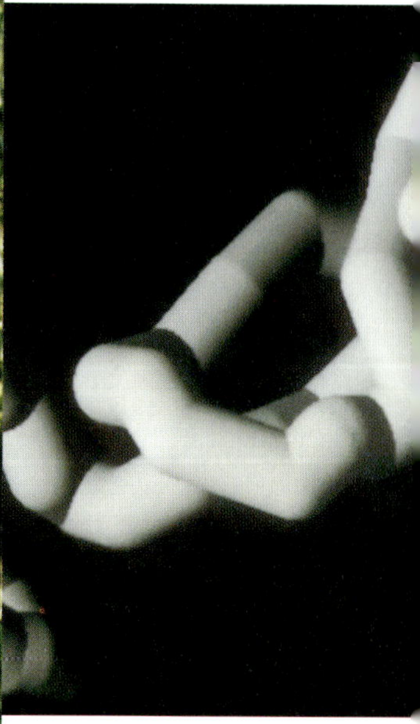

Space-grown crystals.

Scientists are using the near weightlessness (microgravity) of space to grow large crystals of proteins that are important to human health. Crystals grown in space provide more accurate and detailed information about the structure of complex molecules, such as insulin, than crystals grown on Earth. This information will be used to create new and better drugs to treat diseases. Bioengineers also hope to grow tissue patches in the microgravity of space. These patches may be used to repair damaged human tissues, such as heart muscle or bone.

Human research in space.

Astronauts in space and elderly people on Earth experience similar symptoms, such as bone and muscle loss, disturbed sleep patterns, and difficulty with balance. By studying the effects of space travel on volunteer astronauts like Senator John Glenn, scientists hope to learn how to reduce or reverse these symptoms. Their findings may help them learn how to improve the health of elderly people and help spacecraft crews stay healthy during long missions.

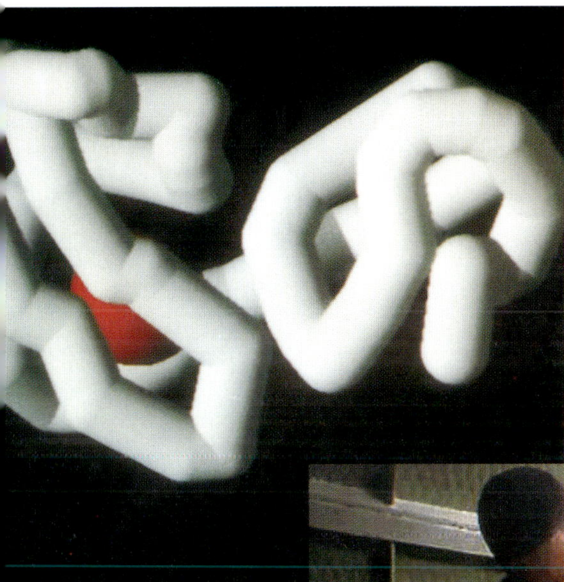

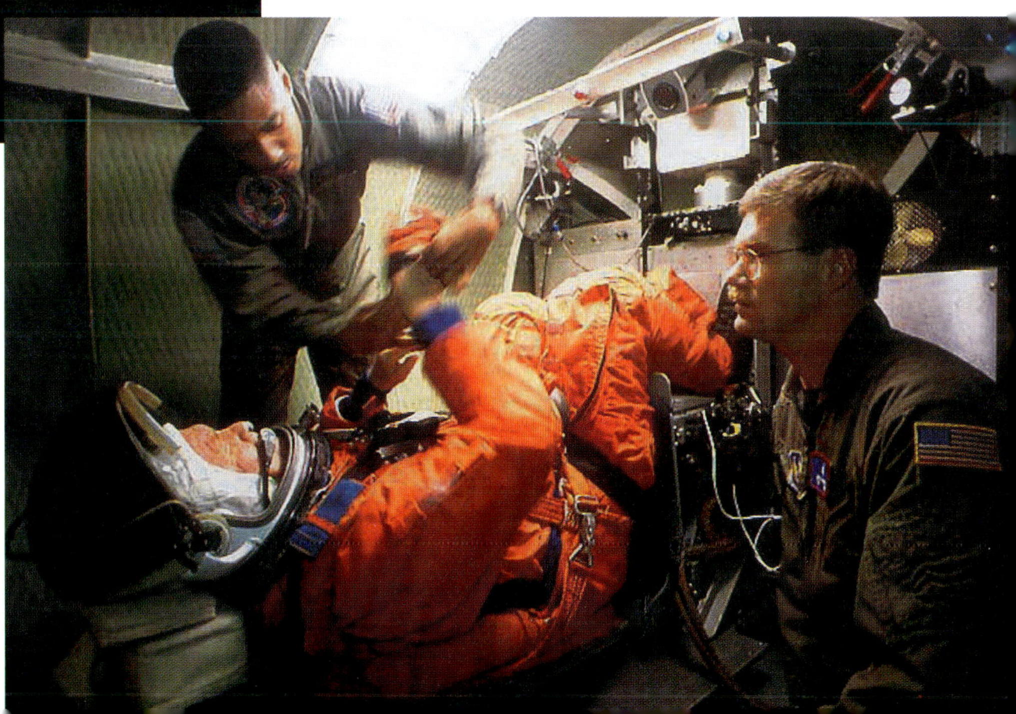

Index

For further reading

Books

Miller, Brandon Marie. *Just What the Doctor Ordered: The History of American Medicine.* People's History series. Minneapolis: Lerner Publications, 1997.

Parker, Steve. *Medical Advances.* 20th Century Innovations series. Austin, TX: Raintree/Steck Vaughn, 1998.

Ritchie, David, et al. *Health and Medicine.* Life in America 100 Years Ago series. Broomall, PA: Chelsea House Publishers, 1995.

Web sites

Medicine through Time
Information about the history of medicine
http://www.bbc.co.uk/education/medicine

The Annenberg/CPB Project Exhibits Collection
Information about aspects of life in the Middle Ages, including medicine
http://www.learner.org/exhibits/middleages